# Together In Love

*Covenant Discipleship With Youth*

David C. Sutherland

**DISCIPLESHIP** RESOURCES

P.O. BOX 840 • NASHVILLE, TENNESSEE 37202-0840

www.discipleshipresources.org

## Dedicated to:

My wife, Pebble

Allan Bruner

Rev. Lamar Davis

## Acknowledgments

First United Methodist Church, Conway, Arkansas

Belmont United Methodist Church, Nashville, Tennessee

Hendrix College, Conway, Arkansas

Cover and book design by Sharon Anderson

ISBN 0-88177-271-2

Library of Congress Catalog Card No. 98-88816

DR271

# Contents

## Part 4: Additional Helps

### Using This Resource

- For background information on Covenant Discipleship Groups, see Part 1.
- For help in developing Covenant Discipleship Groups, see Part 2.
- For help in maintaining Covenant Discipleship Groups, see Part 3.
- For sample forms, covenants, and other additional helps, see Part 4.

# Part 1

Branches
on the Vine

"Just as the branch cannot bear fruit by itself
unless it abides in the vine, neither can you
unless you abide in me."
**John 15:4b**

# Jesus Is the Vine

The image in the first verse of John 15 is vivid, and the message is clear. In this image, the vine is the twisted, gnarled trunk or woody stem of the grape plant that provides support and nourishment to the branches, leaves, and fruit of the plant.

We are called to Jesus Christ in different ways and at different times. Yet the image of a twisted, gnarled grapevine wraps all the different ways and times into one simple statement about our relationship with Christ: Christ is always there as the solid vine that uplifts us, provides our sustenance, and defines our relationship to the earth.

## We Are the Branches

This message that Christ is the vine and that we are the branches is one that we all need to be reminded of; but it is particularly important to youth, who often wither in a world where earthly temptations seem far removed from the presence and support of Christ's love. As youth search for a sense of belonging and yearn for acceptance, it is comforting to hear that Christ is not merely present in our lives but that we are connected to him in a vine and branch relationship.

## Branches That Bear Fruit

Once we are aware of Christ's presence in our lives, we want to respond to his desire for us to be branches that bear good fruit. This urge to respond can be particularly powerful at that time when our awareness of Christ's presence first surfaces.

The problem with our urge to respond is twofold. First, we may not really understand what it means to be a disciple of Christ. Second, it may be difficult to maintain our initial enthusiasm as time passes and as the ways of the world slowly seep back into our daily lives. These problems are compounded for youth because of youth's lack of experience and knowledge. A characteristic of youthful naiveté is the expectation that all problems have quick, simple solutions. So how do we proceed?

The first problem seems easy to solve. We can read the Gospels and study Christ's example. We can pray for guidance. We can ask others for advice and study any of the thousands of Bible studies or spiritual guides.

Eventually, we discover that Christ's commandment goes beyond our individual relationship with Christ. It is also about our relationship with others—we are not the only branches on the vine. We learn that through our relationships with others, our relationship with Christ grows and is strengthened. Thus, bearing fruit is not just about doing good deeds but also about our involvement in the lives of those affected by those good

> "I am the vine, you are the branches."
>
> **John 15:5a**

> "My Father is glorified by this, that you bear much fruit and become my disciples."
>
> **John 15:8**

deeds. By focusing on the fruits of discipleship, our branch's connection to the vine is strengthened.

## Mutual Accountability

Now we return to the second problem—the passage of time and lagging spirits. Recognition of our dependence on Christ and our desire to be a disciple of Christ often comes in a flash, carrying deep emotional power. However, deciding what it means to be a disciple takes time. No matter how strong our initial commitment, that intensity slowly ebbs away.

Our world is a busy place, and our lives are busy and complicated. This is as true for youth as it is for adults. There is often little time for relaxation and sleep, much less time for Christ. Our desire to follow his example is easily pushed to the end of the day and to the back of our minds. Sometimes it is difficult even to remember that we have a commitment to Christ.

Just as our relationship with Christ is realized through caring for others, we also need around us others who live a Christ-centered life. We need others around to help us remember Christ's call and to make sure that Christ is not buried by our busyness.

As adults working with youth in our church, we realize that becoming a disciple of Christ is an ongoing struggle. Not only do youth need to have mentors who are good disciples, but they also need to see those mentors working through the struggles that are part of discipleship. Even more transforming are experiences when youth realize that by their involvement, they can influence the outcomes of some of those adult struggles.

Of course, the issue at hand is one of mutual accountability. The reality of Christian discipleship is that it often consists of unrealized good intentions. Not only do we not always do the things that we know we need to do, but we also do not even do the things we want to do. We need to be surrounded by a community of others striving for similar goals; we need to help one another attain those goals. Christian discipleship outside a community of Christian fellowship rarely succeeds.

## John Wesley and Class Meetings

More than two centuries ago, John Wesley organized Methodist followers into small groups or classes of about a dozen Christians who met each week to help one another become more faithful servants of Jesus Christ. A focus of these meetings was mutual accountability in that each member reported his or her weekly discipleship. The result of the sharing of their successes and failures was stronger disciples.

Wesley understood human nature and understood the difficulties of discipleship. People need structure around which to organize their lives; and the class meetings were an integral part of Wesley's "methods," which led to the name Methodists. If we return to the analogy in John 15, we could say that Wesley's methods were a way of pruning the branches to help them strengthen and bear fruit.

Over the past century, Wesley's early focus on mutual accountability faded away, and the class meetings evolved into today's Sunday school classes and small-group ministries. Mutual accountability may be a part of some of these small groups, but Wesley's original focus has been largely forgotten. What is needed is a model that reminds us of our commitment to discipleship and that helps us evaluate how well we are keeping that commitment.

## Covenant Discipleship Groups

Over the past two decades, Wesleyan scholar David Lowes Watson has revived interest in Wesley's class meetings and their emphasis on mutual accountability. Covenant Discipleship Groups are Watson's modern version of class meetings. They provide an opportunity to grow as disciples for Christians who realize that they need the mutual support and accountability provided by a group of fellow Christians working toward the same goals.

A Covenant Discipleship Group is a group of eight to ten Christians who together develop a covenant that states the ways the members would like to be better disciples. The group meets for about an hour each week to report to one another how well each has done in keeping the covenant during the past week. The covenant contains a list of clauses, each of which relates to some aspect of Christian discipleship. For example, one clause might concern prayer life; another might concern Scripture reading. During a covenant group meeting, the members sit in a circle or around a table. They go through the covenant, clause by clause. The members report how well they kept each clause during the past week. Through account- ability and mutual support, group members grow in their faith and commitment to Christian discipleship.

When they first hear the description of Covenant Discipleship Groups, some people immediately ask how scheduling another hour to talk about Christian discipleship can help. Why should they not spend that hour bearing fruit and actively doing Christian discipleship?

The question is natural and a fair one to ask. The answer lies in our accountability. For example, consider a simple New Year's Day resolution to read a chapter of the Bible every night. How many of us would still be reading every night by the end of February? Or by the end of July?

Now ask yourself how long you would keep this resolution if you shared it with a few good friends who asked you about your reading each week. If you believe that you would keep your resolution longer with the support of a few good friends sharing your goal, then you understand accountability. That shared accountability is what Covenant Discipleship Groups are about. Being a disciple of Jesus Christ is not always easy, and we need to recognize the role that others play in our discipleship.

## The General Rule of Discipleship

Another way Covenant Discipleship Groups follow in the Wesleyan tradi- tion is in their understanding and organization of the acts of discipleship. Where the discipleship of the early class meetings was based on Wesley's General Rules, the covenants of today's groups are based on the General Rule of Discipleship:

*To witness to Jesus Christ in the world and to follow his teachings through acts of compassion, justice, worship, and devotion under the guidance of the Holy Spirit.*

This General Rule reminds us of four aspects of discipleship, each of which is important and necessary. Leading a life of discipleship requires a careful balancing of compassion, justice, worship, and devotion.

One way to emphasize and to remember this delicate balance is to use a Jerusalem cross to display the General Rule. This depiction shows the balance between loving God through works of piety and loving others through works of mercy, as well as the balance between acts of discipleship that are public and those that are private.

## Youth and College Students as Branches That Bear Fruit

Like the adults in our church, the youth in our church have a desire to respond to Christ's call to discipleship. As noted earlier, youth strive to be accepted not only by their peers and by adults but also by Christ.

Like adults, youth also need structure in their lives. At a time when their bodies and minds are maturing at a rapid pace, they need structure and constancy to help them maintain their hold on the world. From the awkward growth spurts of early adolescence to the untried social freedoms of college life, youth need strong, focused guidance from experienced disciples.

Youth need disciples who understand their concerns and desires and who understand the frustration of realizing that wanting to be a Christian disciple is often not enough to make it happen.

## Youth Covenant Discipleship Groups

The aspects of mutual support and accountability that are found in Covenant Discipleship Groups can be as helpful for youth as they are for adults.

Youth Covenant Discipleship Groups may be modified in a variety of ways to meet needs specific to youth. These groups are often formed for very narrowly defined groups of people, such as a specific age group. While an age difference of five years is fairly insignificant among adults, an age difference of five years between two youth can be an almost insurmountable gap.

Another practical issue for youth is transportation. Many youth are dependent on others for transportation. Thus, youth commitment to a Covenant Discipleship Group is often dependent upon the commitment of parents, older siblings, or other relatives.

While Covenant Discipleship Groups are appropriate in a wide variety of settings, several specific opportunities are described in this chapter. Later chapters will further develop these examples and the related changes that are needed to adapt Covenant Discipleship Groups for youth.

*The General Rule of Discipleship:* **To witness to Jesus Christ in the world and to follow his teachings through acts of compassion, justice, worship, and devotion under the guidance of the Holy Spirit.**

## Confirmation Classes

Covenant Discipleship Groups are being used successfully as part of the confirmation program in many local churches. Confirmation is a time of exploring the meaning and commitment of Christian discipleship. The act of forming a covenant around the General Rule of Discipleship and then trying to help one another keep the commitments of the covenant can be an important aspect of the confirmation experience.

Youth Covenant Discipleship Groups have been incorporated into confirmation programs in several ways. Churches that have Sprouts groups for children can easily move youth into Covenant Discipleship Groups at the time of confirmation. One possibility is to offer confirmation youth optional Covenant Discipleship Groups that meet at times separate from other confirmation activities. If your church teaches a short-term confirmation class over a few weeks or months, Covenant Discipleship Groups can be initiated during the regular class and then continued after the completion of other confirmation activities. Churches that have year-long confirmation classes may devote a portion of each session to a Covenant Discipleship Group meeting.

There are two pitfalls to avoid when combining Youth Covenant Discipleship Groups and a confirmation program. If the two types of activities are scheduled separately, youth and their parents may find it difficult to juggle schedules to include both activities. A second problem can arise if a church has a well-established confirmation program whose adult leaders either are not particularly interested in incorporating accountable discipleship into the existing confirmation curriculum or feel unequipped to unify two different programs into one experience. Leaders at local churches that have overcome these potential problems affirm that the combination can make the confirmation process more meaningful to the youth involved.

## Junior and Senior High School Students

Youth Covenant Discipleship Groups can be organized for students in particular grades or for mixed grades. Covenant Discipleship Groups may be a component of United Methodist Youth Fellowship or other youth activities, or they may be planned separately. Youth Covenant Discipleship Groups may even meet during a portion of the Sunday school hour.

Youth Covenant Discipleship Groups can be scheduled in schools where religious organizations meet in the school before or after school hours. Although Covenant Discipleship Groups are rooted in the Wesleyan tradition, the groups need not be restricted to United Methodists or to members of any other particular denomination.

## College Students

Covenant Discipleship Groups for college students are somewhat easier to schedule and organize, since transportation is less of a problem for college students. Since college students are seasonal residents, these groups need to be defined by the academic year. Meeting times and membership may need to change each semester, thus placing more pressure on organizers to make decisions quickly and more frequently.

But when the chief priests and the scribes saw the amazing things that he [Jesus] did, and heard the children crying out in the temple, "Hosanna to the Son of David," they became angry and said to him, "Do you hear what these are saying?" Jesus said to them, "Yes; have you never read, 'Out of the mouths of infants and nursing babies you have prepared praise for yourself'?"
**Matthew 21:15-16**

# Part
# 2

## Preparing for Healthy Branches

"If you keep my commandments, you will abide in my love, just as I have kept my Father's commandments and abide in his love."
**John 15:10**

# Understanding Covenant Discipleship Groups

Jesus' commandments are stated clearly and simply in Matthew 22:37-40. We are asked to love the Lord with all our heart, soul, and mind; and we are asked to love our neighbors as ourselves. It sounds so simple.

Of course, we realize that even if the commandments are simple, we still need day-to-day reminders to follow through on our desire to keep those commandments. And Covenant Discipleship Groups may appear to be a reasonably easy way to keep those commandments foremost in our thoughts and practices.

But the world in which we live teaches us to be skeptical about anything that appears to be simple or easy. That skepticism is one lesson that youth seem to learn very early in their lives. Will they appreciate the concept of Covenant Discipleship Groups and believe that they might be helpful?

Yes, youth will understand if you will follow the lead of Jesus and begin by teaching the basics. The concepts of Christian discipleship, mutual accountability, commitment, and covenant provide a firm foundation for understanding Covenant Discipleship Groups.

## Christian Discipleship

The first basic idea is understanding what is meant by Christian discipleship. The passage from Matthew is as simple as it sounds. Christian disciples love the Lord with their heart, soul, and mind; Christian disciples love their neighbors as themselves.

We make these commandments complicated when we try to state exactly how we should go about following them. We also forget that understanding evolves over time. Subtleties are not for beginners. Youth who are just beginning to develop in their discipleship are rarely ready for explanations that make perfect sense to experienced disciples.

Youth understand these commandments as they are stated. Rather than attempt a detailed interpretation of these commandments, simply ask the youth to explain what they think the commandments mean. They may leave out details that are important, or they may completely ignore some aspects that we associate with Christian discipleship, but it will be evident that they understand. More important, the youth will have processed this passage for themselves and thus will have incorporated this message from Jesus into their own Christian journey.

If we read the verses of Matthew that precede this passage, the simplicity of Jesus' commandments also can be interpreted as a warning about our discipleship. In this passage, the Pharisees are questioning Jesus about the

He [Jesus] said to him, " 'You shall love the Lord your God with all your heart, and with all your soul, and with all your mind.' This is the greatest and first commandment. And a second is like it: 'You shall love your neighbor as yourself.' On these two commandments hang all the law and the prophets."
**Matthew 22:37-40**

law. In their questioning, they intend to trick Jesus into saying something that contradicts Jewish law. They ask him what is necessary to lead a religious life. His simple answer reminds us that sometimes we add on so many complications and details that the rules become an end in themselves. These "add ons" may help hide the limitations in our own Christian discipleship, just as the Pharisees were blinded by their own inflexible view of Jewish law.

## Mutual Accountability

Mutual accountability may be a new concept for youth. They may be familiar with the two words individually but may have never heard them used together.

For youth, the word *accountability* is often tied to relationships with authority figures. Youth understand what is meant when a parent or teacher tells them that they will be held accountable for their actions. Accountability is understood as responsibility combined with an authority figure's monitoring of that responsibility.

Youth also understand accountability in terms of their participation in organized groups. These groups might be a choir, a band, an athletic team, UMYF, a Sunday school class, or any other organization. Again, youth understand accountability as individual responsibility to these groups. Some youth will think of that accountability as shared responsibilities that the group members have to one another. These youth have an excellent understanding of mutual accountability.

However, most youth will understand group responsibility as responsibility to the group as its own entity or to the group leader. Even though they are overlooking the idea of shared responsibility to one another, the understanding is closer to the idea of mutual accountability than in parent-child or teacher-student relationships, where most youth cannot see past the authority issue.

Many youth will best understand mutual accountability in terms of how they and their friends relate to one another. They understand their responsibilities to their friends, as well as their dependence on one another to help hold the group together.

An extreme example of youth's understanding of mutual accountability is seen in gangs. One pastor involved in prison ministry reported that he had successfully used Covenant Discipleship Groups with young ex-gang members. Although these youth had difficulties relating to almost every aspect of what we would call a normal Christian lifestyle, they responded naturally to the idea of mutual accountability. Accountability to the members of the gang was an important part of their past.

A final model of mutual accountability for youth is a project group in school. One change in education in the past decade is the increased amount of time students spend working on projects in small groups. Students see a group project as a shared responsibility. The group members must work together and help one another complete the task. Watch one of these groups in action. After each member has been sent away to complete an individual component of the project, you will hear students ask one another if they have completed their assigned tasks. They are holding one another accountable.

Youth have been involved in many group projects in school. They have experienced successful groups and groups that were dismal failures. They understand many of the problems inherent in group dynamics. They know what can go wrong, because they have been there before. Later, we will see how these experiences can help youth prepare for problems that may arise in Covenant Discipleship Groups.

## Commitment

The level of commitment of the Covenant Discipleship Group members affects every aspect of the group interaction and is a crucial issue in whether a Covenant Discipleship Group is successful. Youth understand commitment, but their ability to accurately measure their own level of commitment is limited. Pressure from peers or adult leaders can strongly affect how youth interpret or make commitments.

Youth understand that they will be required to keep some commitments and will not be required to keep others. When parents tell their son or daughter that they will hold him or her accountable to a particular commitment, the child can usually predict whether the parents are serious about following through. When youth make a commitment, they intuitively analyze the dynamics of the situation and the people involved. Youth often more accurately evaluate the desires of others than they do their own desires.

Youth make commitments for different reasons. Some commitments are made because they are important to the youth, and some commitments are made because the youth realize that the commitments are important to someone else. Youth are willing to go along because it is easier to agree than to disagree; youth generally do not want to stand out or to appear to be different.

Another issue affecting commitment is time. Youth respond to the immediacy of the situation. Like many adults, youth do not always evaluate the requirements of a long-term commitment. Ask a group of youth if they would like to perform a play at an upcoming children's worship service. They might respond enthusiastically, "Yes!" Now imagine how many of them will happily attend the third or fourth rehearsal.

Leaders need to realize that the initial enthusiasm will not get them through several long rehearsal sessions. Commitment to a Covenant Discipleship Group works in the same way. The initial commitment often should be viewed as a short-term commitment. Leaders and successful group dynamics will help sustain that commitment for the long term.

As long as adult leaders understand these differences in commitment, a Covenant Discipleship Group should be successful. Leaders should not expect youth's commitment to a Covenant Discipleship Group to be any different from their other commitments. Leaders will have to work on sustaining youth commitment. With the right guidance, the initial commitment often grows into a long-term commitment.

I establish my covenant with you [Noah and all living creatures], that never again shall all flesh be cut off by the waters of a flood, and never again shall there be a flood to destroy the earth.
**Genesis 9:11**

## Covenant

Covenant is the concept in Covenant Discipleship that youth have the least experience with. Youth may think of a covenant as a contract, but they have little awareness of the biblical importance of covenant relationships. Another complication is that the term *covenant* is used in two ways. First is the biblical story of God's covenant with God's people. Second is the covenant that people make with one another in order to structure their response to God's covenant.

The idea of a covenant first appears explicitly in the Noah story in Genesis. Youth may not remember all the details of the Noah story, but they will remember the rainbow as a sign of God's promise, or covenant, with all living creatures to never again destroy the world with a flood.

Later in Genesis, God told Abraham that God would be God to him and to all of his descendants. In Exodus, Moses referred to the Ten Commandments as the book of the covenant; and the people responded with a pledge of obedience to God. Much of the history in the Old Testament is a history of that covenant with God and the cycle of the people alternately keeping and breaking the covenant.

In Jeremiah we hear of a promise of a new covenant that will restore our covenant relationship with God, and our sin will be forgotten. Christians understand this to be the new covenant that Jesus refers to in the Last Supper with the disciples. This new covenant is the grace of Christ Jesus that we celebrate in the ritual of Communion. In fact, youth may be surprised to know that the complete title of the New Testament in the New Revised Standard Version of the Bible is "The New Covenant Commonly Called The New Testament of Our Lord and Savior Jesus Christ."

So in many ways, the Bible can be thought of as the story of the covenant relationship between God and God's people. Christian discipleship can then be described as a way of life in which we follow the commandments of Jesus as a response to God's covenant with us. Covenant Discipleship Group leaders may want to spend some time teaching the biblical understanding of God's covenant relationship with us.

God's covenant with the people of God is not the covenant that is the focus of Covenant Discipleship Groups. The Covenant Discipleship Group covenant follows from our realization that being a Christian disciple is harder than it appears. We may want to be Christian disciples, but obstacles—distractions, lack of time, and lack of energy—keep appearing. How can we maintain our focus on following Jesus? We need others to help us keep the focus.

Covenant Discipleship is a way of structuring our response to God's gift of grace. The covenant in this context is a written document that lists the ways in which a group of people desire to live out the commandments of Jesus. The people in the group covenant work together to help one another follow Christ's example through mutual accountability.

The covenant serves two purposes. First, it is a statement of how the group members interpret Christ's call to follow his commandments. Second, the covenant states exactly how the group members plan to live out this interpretation. For example, a covenant might contain a statement that the group members will pray each day, including the other group members in their prayers. So we know that the group agrees that they should be praying

> I will establish my covenant between me and you [Abraham], and your off-spring after you throughout their generations, for an everlasting covenant, to be God to you and to your offspring after you.
>
> **Genesis 17:7**

> And Moses wrote down all the words of the LORD. . . . Then he took the book of the covenant, and read it in the hearing of the people; and they said, "All that the LORD has spoken we will do, and we will be obedient."
>
> **Exodus 24:4a, 7**

and that they state their commitment to do so each day. A later section will give specific suggestions about the format and content of covenants for Youth Covenant Discipleship Groups (see page 25).

## Organizing a Covenant Discipleship Group

Many of the issues involved in organizing Covenant Discipleship Groups are those found in organizing any youth activity: Who is the target audience? Are adult leaders available and willing? How can the church support the groups? Can the groups find available time slots in which to meet? Will youth have transportation? Although the answers to these questions overlap, each will be discussed separately.

### Determining Age Level and Format

One of the first decisions in organizing a Youth Covenant Discipleship Group is to determine the age level of the participants and the format of the group meetings. In general, junior high youth, senior high youth, and college students should be considered separate age groups. This is especially important if the leaders and youth involved have not had prior experience with Covenant Discipleship. It is easier to have successful Covenant Discipleship Groups if the age range is fairly narrow. Remember that a youth in seventh grade and a youth in eleventh grade have widely different social and educational experiences and interests.

In some situations Covenant Discipleship Group participation will be limited to a small number of youth, and it will not be practical to separate youth according to age. Having groups of mixed age can certainly be a positive experience and is more likely to succeed when the youth are comfortable being together.

Another exception to keeping the age range narrow is when some youth have prior experience with Covenant Discipleship. These experienced youth can serve leadership roles in mixed-age groups. This can be especially beneficial if the experienced youth are older than the rest of the youth in the Covenant Discipleship Group.

The format of the group may help determine the age level of the youth involved. The major formats of a Youth Covenant Discipleship Group are
- independent Covenant Discipleship Groups
- integrated Covenant Discipleship Groups
- continuation Covenant Discipleship Groups

Independent Covenant Discipleship Groups are groups that are formed specifically as Covenant Discipleship Groups. Group members may see one another as a group only during Covenant Discipleship Group meetings. These groups work well for senior high students and college students because these groups are generally more focused and mature and are therefore able to concentrate on Covenant Discipleship for a more extended period of time. These age groups are also less likely to be dependent on others for transportation.

Integrated Covenant Discipleship Groups exist as part of another regular activity such as Sunday school classes, confirmation classes, or UMYF. The

The days are surely coming, says the LORD, when I will make a new covenant with the house of Israel and the house of Judah. It will not be like the covenant that I made with their ancestors when I took them by the hand to bring them out of the land of Egypt—a covenant that they broke. . . . But this is the covenant that I will make with the house of Israel after those days, says the LORD: I will put my law within them, and I will write it on their hearts; and I will be their God, and they shall be my people. . . . for I will forgive their iniquity, and remember their sin no more.

Jeremiah 31:31-32a, 33, 34b

group already exists for some other purpose, and the Covenant Discipleship Group is simply one of the components that the group members experience together. This format is especially good for gradually easing younger youth into the Covenant Discipleship process.

For example, consider a confirmation class of seventh graders who meet once a week for an hour. Perhaps only fifteen to twenty minutes of the hour will be devoted to Covenant Discipleship Groups. Rather than beginning with a complete covenant covering all four components of the General Rule of Discipleship, the youth can focus on one discipleship area at a time. Over time, all discipleship areas will be discussed; but progress will be slower and more narrowly focused than in a stand-alone group.

Continuation Covenant Discipleship Groups are formed from groups of youth who have completed some long-term group activity such as a confirmation class, a youth DISCIPLE Bible study group, or a Chrysalis event. If the group has developed a close relationship and wishes to continue meeting, a Covenant Discipleship Group is a way for group members to continue to grow together in their Christian discipleship.

## Determining Leadership

Once the age level and format have been decided, leadership needs to be determined. In most Youth Covenant Discipleship Groups, it is important to have adult participation in the group. Adult leadership is especially important in junior high Covenant Discipleship Groups because of the inexperience and lack of maturity of the students. Adult leadership is advised even in Covenant Discipleship Groups with college students, although college students who have previous experience with Covenant Discipleship may serve as leaders in groups of less-experienced students.

Adults serve in Youth Covenant Discipleship Groups in the following capacities:
- monitor
- participant
- facilitator

Adult leaders should monitor interactions and generally maintain control. In some cases with less mature youth, the leader should be prepared to serve as an intervener or even a disciplinarian, although the mere presence of an adult will usually suffice. Church building rules or security policies also may require the presence of one or more adults.

Adult leaders should participate fully as members of the Covenant Discipleship Group. The adult leader should model mutual accountability and good discipleship. Youth need to know that adults struggle daily with their discipleship just as youth do. Adult modeling helps youth understand that Christian discipleship is a lifelong journey. Participation by the adult leaders also helps preserve the nature of mutual accountability. Youth will grow from the shared experience of mutual accountability with an adult, as contrasted with their more typical experience of accountability to adults in positions of authority.

Adult leaders need to take care not to be overly zealous or successful in following the covenant. Adult participation should model individual struggle

While they were eating, he took a loaf of bread, and after blessing it he broke it, gave it to them, and said, "Take; this is my body." Then he took a cup, and after giving thanks he gave it to them, and all of them drank from it. He said to them, "This is my blood of the [new] covenant, which is poured out for many."

Mark 14:22-24

with discipleship rather than provide an intimidating report from a "successful" disciple. Adults may need to focus on those parts of the covenant with which they themselves struggle. The later section on writing the covenant will return to this issue.

Adult leaders should be prepared to facilitate group dynamics and to encourage full participation of all group members. Shy, quiet members may need encouragement to participate; more exuberant youth may need help staying on task. Youth will be pleased with individual successes in keeping parts of the covenant. But they will need help handling frustrations in their attempts to keep other parts of the covenant. Adults can help the youth examine their frustrations in a caring way that de-emphasizes failure and emphasizes that goals are works in progress. They should be prepared to offer simple ways to make the goals more manageable and easy to remember. Youth need to understand that not one of us is perfect and that we often need help accepting the gift of Christ's grace.

What kinds of adults should be recruited as leaders? Begin with two basic criteria: Leaders should enjoy working with youth, and leaders should appreciate the role of mutual accountability in their own Christian discipleship.

In a local church, the organizer should meet with adults who volunteer regularly with youth. Explain Covenant Discipleship and ask for volunteers. If adult Covenant Discipleship Groups meet in the church, the organizer should meet with those groups as well to see if there are members interested in helping form Youth Covenant Discipleship Groups.

If adults interested in leading Youth Covenant Discipleship Groups have little experience with Covenant Discipleship, perhaps an experienced covenant group member will agree to meet with the group for one or two meetings to get the group started. Another possibility is to use two adults in each Youth Covenant Discipleship Group—one who has Covenant Discipleship experience and one who has experience working with youth. An older adult who would be an unlikely participant in other youth activities may be well-received in the Youth Covenant Discipleship Group setting.

On a college campus, the chaplain's office or Wesley Foundation ministers should be able to suggest potential leadership. Faculty and staff who regularly participate in campus worship or other religious activities on campus are all potential participants in College Covenant Discipleship Groups.

Integrated Covenant Discipleship Groups and continuation Youth Covenant Discipleship Groups may have leadership built into the groups. Using the existing leadership is a good idea as long as those people are interested in modeling discipleship through mutual accountability.

## Developing a Support Network

Although Youth and College Covenant Discipleship Groups function independently, developing a wider support network for the group members is beneficial. Support may come from the following groups:
- family members and friends of the youth involved
- church youth program or campus ministry program
- church or campus ministry staff
- congregation

Support from the family and friends of youth involved in Covenant Discipleship Groups is important because the actual living out of the youth's Christian discipleship will take place at home and in school. For younger youth, involvement of parents is even more crucial. Parents should be invited to an orientation session and may be asked to make a commitment to support their children's desires to become better Christian disciples. A sample of a parent commitment form is found on page 45.

For younger youth a commitment to be a part of any program is a commitment by the youth's family. Someone will need to provide transportation to group meetings, and the family schedule will need to be flexible enough to accommodate the Covenant Discipleship Group schedule.

Family involvement in the commitment extends beyond scheduling. Commitments to prayer at meals, Bible study or meditation time, and even recycling may be included in a Youth Covenant Discipleship Group covenant; and each of these involves the support and cooperation of the youth's family. Posting a laminated copy of the covenant on the refrigerator door or on the family message board is one way to visually remind the family of the covenant commitment. Sharing in some of the covenant commitments will strengthen the entire family.

Support from the church youth program or campus ministry program is important, even though not all youth will be involved in a Covenant Discipleship Group. Youth need the support of their peers, and they need to know that their commitment is respected by others. Likewise, peer support provides an opportunity for the Covenant Discipleship Group members to minister to other youth. Youth Covenant Discipleship Group members may want to organize UMYF sessions about their covenants. They may want to provide leadership for additional worship or service opportunities for the youth program.

Church staff or campus ministry staff support is also important to providing a strong support system to Covenant Discipleship Group members. Even more important, the staff can assure that Covenant Discipleship Groups are incorporated and integrated into the larger programmatic, planning, and scheduling calendars of the church or campus ministry program.

Congregational support can be equally important to the youth in Covenant Discipleship Groups. Some churches celebrate a covenant Sunday when adult Covenant Discipleship Groups are begun. Many churches also regularly commission various programs and ministries during worship services—for example, Sunday school teachers, volunteers-in-mission teams, or work trips. The commissioning of Youth Covenant Discipleship Groups is equally appropriate and helps youth feel integrated into the life of the church. A sample commissioning service is found on page 52.

If multiple Youth Covenant Discipleship Groups are meeting in a particular church, the leaders should meet with one another occasionally. It can even be helpful to schedule quarterly worship, service, or social events for the combined groups.

### Developing the Schedule and Budget

Independent and continuation Covenant Discipleship Groups usually meet once a week for about an hour. Smaller groups may need less time, but one hour is generally a realistic minimum time allotment. Because of youth transportation needs it can be beneficial to schedule meetings before or after other youth programs or during other adult programs. It is probably most convenient if the church is the location of group meetings.

Integrated Covenant Discipleship Groups require substantial changes from the basic format of one-hour meetings. Begin by deciding how much of the scheduled meeting time can be devoted to the Covenant Discipleship component. Fifteen to twenty minutes is the minimum time required for a group of about eight youth to have a meaningful Covenant Discipleship Group session.

The next step is for the leaders and participants to realize that the entire covenant cannot realistically be covered in fifteen to twenty minutes. The covenant needs to be broken into several distinct parts. As will be discussed in a later section, the covenants are usually written in four parts that correspond to the four components of the the General Rule of Discipleship.

The integrated Covenant Discipleship Group may focus on one section of the covenant for four or five consecutive meetings. This gives the youth time to practice individual aspects of their discipleship for an extended time. This approach works especially well for younger youth and confirmation classes. It is particularly effective if the other components of the meeting time can focus on related aspects during that same period of time. For example, consider a yearlong confirmation class that meets during Sunday school time. The month when the covenant focus is on acts of devotion could be a month when the confirmation lessons also focus on the role of acts of devotion in a Christian's life.

College Covenant Discipleship Groups are usually scheduled differently. Since college students are more independent, Covenant Discipleship Groups should meet at times and places most convenient for the students involved. Late evenings (8:00 P.M. to 11:00 P.M.) are popular times for college students. Students may want to meet in the chapel or the religious life space, but dormitory rooms and library study rooms are equally popular.

It is helpful for Covenant Discipleship Group leaders at colleges to participate in activity fairs that are scheduled during the week before classes get started. Brochures describing Covenant Discipleship should be available. A sample appears on pages 42-43. Brochures also should be available in the religious life center, chaplain's office, or Wesley Foundation. Also, ask to make an announcement at the first chapel service of the academic year.

Creation of a website for Covenant Discipleship Groups can be an important way to communicate with college students. If leaders are not comfortable with creating web pages, it is usually not difficult to locate a student who is willing to convert the materials in a brochure into a web page. The web page should include a link to the General Board of Discipleship website at **http://www.gbod.org.** The GBOD website provides additional information about accountable discipleship ministries.

Budget requirements for Covenant Discipleship Groups are minimal. In addition to staff time and building usage, the following optional items should be considered in the budget process:
- printing or photocopying of written materials
- postage for mailed communications

- laminating of small copies of covenants
- refreshments for the orientation session and quarterly meetings
- subscriptions for devotional materials
- a retreat or service project

## Planning the Orientation Meeting and Assigning Groups

Once all of the background work has been completed, it is time to plan an orientation session for youth and parents. Before the orientation session, youth and parents should have received a packet containing a brochure, a copy of a sample covenant, and a commitment form for parents. Youth also should have heard announcements and brief presentations during Sunday school classes and UMYF meetings.

The orientation session should serve the following purposes:
- Explain the Youth Covenant Discipleship Group format.
- Develop the biblical basis for Covenant Discipleship.
- Introduce the adult leadership.
- Generate excitement for growing in Christian discipleship.
- Obtain commitments from youth and parents.
- Have a fun experience involving youth and their parents.

An example of a complete orientation session is included on pages 46-48. Each of the purposes outlined above is served by one or more parts of the sample session. At the conclusion of the orientation session, the leaders should be in a position to obtain commitments from youth who want to join a Covenant Discipleship Group.

Once the youth have made their commitments, they can be assigned to actual groups. Each Covenant Discipleship Group should have between five and ten members. Smaller groups usually work better for younger youth. Smaller groups are also important if the group is an integrated Covenant Discipleship Group, since a limited amount of time is available each session for the Covenant Discipleship Group component.

Various Youth Covenant Discipleship Groups can meet at different times throughout the week, but it may be much easier for parents and staff if the groups meet at a common time and place. This also provides more flexibility for the leaders. If one of the groups is poorly attended on a particular day, then the rest of the group may choose to join another group for that one session. If individuals are simply not fitting into their groups, it is much easier to shift membership around if the groups meet at the same time. It is also easier to plan service or worship experiences for the combined groups.

Having multiple groups meeting at the same time also provides a way to stretch experienced adult leadership. Perhaps a church has one leader who has had experience leading a Youth Covenant Discipleship Group, but there are several people willing to be leaders if they have experienced help. The church may want to schedule several small Youth Covenant Discipleship Groups to meet at the same time and to assign the interested volunteers as leaders. The experienced leader can then float from group to group as needed. The new leaders know that help is available if needed.

Orientation and scheduling usually work differently in college settings. The orientation meeting can be much shorter and can consist of verbal explanations by the prospective group leaders. A sample orientation meeting for College Covenant Discipleship Groups is found on pages 50-51. Note how it has been derived from the model of the youth orientation session but is more direct and to the point. One of the main purposes of the college orientation session is to arrange meeting times. In a few minutes, college students can usually regroup themselves into smaller Covenant Discipleship Groups with agreeable meeting times.

One way to facilitate that regrouping is to include a request for preferred meeting times in the brochure that invites students to the orientation meeting. Leaders can select tentative meeting times in advance that match student requests and that fit their own schedules. During the orientation session, these times can be offered as meeting times.

## Starting a Covenant Discipleship Group

The next steps in the creation of a Youth or College Covenant Discipleship Group are developing the covenant and conducting the initial meeting of the group.

### Developing the Covenant

Thus far, we have spent a lot of time talking in general terms about the Covenant Discipleship Group covenant. Now we will focus on the specific contents of a covenant and how to write it. The group covenant is a collective promise to one another of what the group's members intend to do to be better disciples of Jesus Christ. Essentially, the covenant is a list of goals for a week in the life of the Covenant Discipleship Group member.

Covenants are usually divided into three parts: the introduction, the clauses, and the conclusion. The introduction, or preamble, is a statement of purpose for the Covenant Discipleship Group. It often includes a statement explaining why the group is making a covenant and what the commitment is to one another. The clauses are the explicitly stated goals for discipleship. The conclusion contains a pledge of commitment and a statement of the role of grace in that commitment. It may be helpful to examine the sample covenants on pages 54 and 55 as we walk through the process of creating a covenant.

One way to write a covenant would be for the group members to meet and start listing things each of them would like to do to develop into better Christian disciples. Then the group has ownership of the covenant, and clauses of particular interest to group members will be included. This is how adult groups often proceed. However, this method has problems, particularly with youth.

One problem is that the list may turn out to be random, incomplete, or uneven in its coverage of different aspects of discipleship. Two different discussions with youth volunteering suggestions for the covenant might yield two extremely different lists, each with its own focus or thrust as generated in that discussion, and each omitting important areas of discipleship.

I [the Lord] will make for you a covenant on that day with the wild animals, the birds of the air, and the creeping things of the ground; and I will abolish the bow, the sword, and war from the land; and I will make you lie down in safety. And I will take you for my wife forever; I will take you for my wife in righteousness and in justice, in steadfast love, and in mercy. I will take you for my wife in faithfulness; and you shall know the LORD.

**Hosea 2:18-20**

Following the General Rule of Discipleship, as discussed in Part 1, can solve the problem of uneven discipleship. The rule is as follows: To witness to Jesus Christ in the world and to follow his teachings through acts of compassion, justice, worship, and devotion under the guidance of the Holy Spirit.

This General Rule reminds us of four basic components of discipleship. The rule, along with the Jerusalem cross labeled as shown, is a modern version of John Wesley's General Rules for how to live a complete, balanced life of Christian discipleship.

In our Christian discipleship, there is a tension between our public actions and our private actions. Likewise there is a tension between works of mercy (loving others) and works of piety (loving God). Combining these two concepts results in an understanding of discipleship as having four basic components:

- Acts of Compassion are private works of mercy.
- Acts of Devotion are private works of piety.
- Acts of Justice are public works of mercy.
- Acts of Worship are public works of piety.

This understanding incorporates our Wesleyan heritage and serves as a template for writing Covenant Discipleship Group covenants that lead to a life of balanced discipleship. An unavoidable part of our discipleship is the tension created by trying to balance these parts of discipleship.

Examine the sample covenants to see how this template serves as a practical model for discipleship. Additional examples of each of the four types of Christian acts appear on pages 56–59 and ideas for putting these suggestions into practice appear in Part 3.

Another problem in developing the covenant is that its preparation is cumbersome and delays the beginning of what will be the typical Covenant Discipleship Group meeting. A common perception is that all this preliminary stuff is keeping the group from actually doing something. High energy levels or short attention spans may lead to frustration or boredom before the group even reaches the point of having an actual covenant meeting.

Youth want to do something rather than to talk about doing something. A workable solution is to begin the Covenant Discipleship Group by adopting a short, simple covenant that already exists. At this point in most of the youth's lives, the habit, or discipline, of practicing good discipleship is more important than discussions about what makes good discipleship.

Begin with one of the sample covenants on pages 54–55. If needed, make minor changes to tailor the covenant to the particulars of your group. Then get started. Notice how many of the clauses are written so simply that they appear vague. This is an advantage because it allows the youth to work through the ways in which particular aspects of discipleship are relevant to their individual lives.

For example, consider the clause, "We will avoid sins of the tongue." What does this mean? Ask the youth what they think it means. (This clause was written by college students seeking to avoid lying, swearing, gossiping, and using sarcasm.) A discussion of this clause will generate lots of good, high-energy conversation and perhaps differences of opinion; it will also allow each group or each individual to interpret the clause personally. The group will learn that one individual may work at controlling the use of foul language, and another may try hard not to gossip as much. One simple clause allows the group to get started yet encourages individual growth in unique ways.

Another advantage to simple, clearly written clauses is that they level the playing field for group members. Members of a Covenant Discipleship Group are at different places in their Christian journey, and adult leaders, in particular, can easily overwhelm youth with their own, more detailed discipleship goals.

For example, consider the clause about praying daily. Around the Covenant Discipleship Group, the interpretation of this clause may range from the leader who keeps a detailed daily prayer journal to the youth who rarely remembers to pray at all. The goal here is not to reduce the clauses to the lowest common denominator, but to provide a flexible framework for individual variety in levels of discipleship. As the initial covenant is continually discussed and reinterpreted, the time may arrive when the youth are ready to write a more individualized covenant for their group. The writing of this covenant grows out of the habit of discipleship, and the prospect of writing the covenant never appears frustrating or overwhelming.

The sample covenants (or your adapted version) can be used in the publicity for the groups and should be included as part of the orientation session. Youth and parents both respond well to a situation when they understand exactly what their commitment involves.

College students also may profit from adopting prewritten covenants. The college cycle of semesters or terms consists of short, intense periods of activity. Groups may have to reorganize with each schedule change, and students may want to limit the time spent writing or adopting the covenant. A prewritten covenant is more flexible as students move in and out of Covenant Discipleship Groups as semesters change. Once again, college students can make adaptations to the covenant as the need develops.

## Conducting the Initial Meeting

The youth have attended the orientation session. They have committed to joining a Covenant Discipleship Group. They have seen the initial covenant. It is time for the first Covenant Discipleship Group meeting. What's next? At a minimum, leaders need to accomplish the following in the first meeting:
- Set ground rules in the context of grace.
- Model how Covenant Discipleship Group meetings are conducted.
- Read the covenant together.
- Sign the covenant.

Often youth can be nervous or edgy when they do not know exactly what to expect or how to proceed. Remind them that God loves them regardless of how well their efforts at discipleship are going. No one will be keeping score, and no one should be afraid or ashamed to talk about his or her intentions. Grace is a gift from God, and our discipleship is one of our gifts in return.

Discussion of grace sets the context for reminding the youth how to treat one another. Remind them that mutual support and accountability imply respect and trust. Group members need to respect individual failures and struggles along with celebrating successes. Group members need to trust that information will be treated confidentially. Realistically, confidentiality is one of the greatest challenges for Covenant Discipleship Groups.

Remind the youth that you are a participant as well and that you will ask them to share in the leadership roles. They will need to be good listeners as well as contributors. Conclude this portion of discussion with prayer.

After talking about the ground rules, the leader should describe how the group meetings will be conducted. Groups often begin by praying and then reading the introduction to the covenant in unison. Do these two things. Then select one of the clauses in the covenant and let each member practice responding to how well he or she kept this clause during the past week.

It is important not to intimidate the youth at this point. Keep the tone serious but light. Start with one of the easiest clauses. Or start with a clause with which you have not had success recently. After the group has responded, ask them to talk about the issues raised by the clause. Is it an easy one for them to keep or a difficult one? How can they help one another work on the clause?

Youth need practical suggestions about how to satisfy many of the clauses. It may be necessary to limit the initial meetings to a few selected items in the covenant or to one part of the covenant, because initially it is more important to keep the focus as directed as possible. Explicit examples of how to moti-vate or direct efforts toward individual clauses appear in Part 3.

There generally is not time for extended group discussion following each member's response to each clause. For the most part, there need not be a lot of commenting. It will be necessary to move forward at a steady pace for the group to cover the entire list of clauses in the allotted time.

At the end of the meeting time, ask each youth to sign and date a copy of the covenant for each person. Ask the youth to take their copy home and place it where they will see it every day. One suggestion is that they place it in their Bibles and then place their Bibles on their bedside table or dresser. Tell them that their own signatures remind them of their commitment, and the signatures of the others remind them that they are not alone.

Close by reading the covenant conclusion in unison and leading the group in prayer. Many groups enjoy sharing a benediction together. Suggestions include singing the song "Sanctuary" (found in many Christian songbooks) or saying a biblical benediction. Ask if anyone wishes to volunteer to lead the opening prayer at the next meeting.

# Part 3

## Nurturing Healthy Branches

Bear one another's burdens, and in this way
you will fulfill the law of Christ.
**Galatians 6:2**

# Participating in a Covenant Discipleship Group

## Stimulating Discussion and Participation

One key to a successful Covenant Discipleship Group is stimulating discussion about discipleship without losing sight of the covenant or the group's progress through it. An analogy is a classroom setting where interaction is desired, but the emphasis is on round-robin reading.

Leaders should be flexible enough to allow back-and-forth discussion while gently continuing to move through the covenant and around the group. With many groups, there will be clauses that move quickly around the group, with youth briefly saying, "Yes, I did that this week." These short answers can be positive parts of the process because they can create a feeling of movement in the discussion. Quick positive answers can be especially encouraging after a slow-moving, difficult clause has finally made it around the group.

Quick yes answers also identify clauses in the covenant where group members can focus on strengthening their discipleship. Use this success to motivate movement to a more serious commitment. For example, if everyone is praying each day, then the group can consider specific ways to make their prayer time more meaningful or focused.

Quick no answers also can be dealt with in a positive way. It is important that the youth do not perceive these no answers as failures. Perhaps the group has taken on too great a challenge. Ask the youth to think how they might divide a goal into smaller pieces that are more realistic. For example, if youth are having difficulty remembering to bless the food at meals, then they may need to begin with meals at home and work toward more public situations.

Another approach is to focus on group effort rather than on individual efforts. For example, if youth say that they have not volunteered to participate in worship, then the group can talk about how the youth can participate in worship. Leaders should be prepared to offer realistic suggestions as needed. The youth could decide to volunteer to be ushers or to help serve Communion as a group activity. The group approach builds on mutual accountability and is a positive way to acknowledge the importance of group members to one another's success in keeping the covenant.

A series of quick no answers also may indicate that youth simply do not understand the clause or how it relates to their lives. Youth may need specific examples to help explain the meaning or implications of some clauses. Acts of justice often fall into this category. Youth may not think of many instances of prejudice as prejudice unless the issue is negative and concerns race or gender.

Leaders may look for examples from group members' lives to use as parables through which to teach about justice. Ask the youth if they know anyone at school who gets laughed at by other students because of being different in some way. Leaders may need to describe a hypothetical scenario. Use this scenario to spark the participants' memories about similar situations in their own lives. Help them understand that prejudice comes in many forms.

Youth also may not know how to respond to injustice or prejudice when they do recognize it. They may not understand speaking out against an injustice as anything except standing up loudly and publicly for the person involved. Help the youth see that a first step is simply their recognition that prejudice is involved in the situation. A second step might be for them to avoid participating in the behavior. Talking about the situation with a few friends may begin the process of eliminating the injustice. Development of discipleship may take radical steps at times; but often our development requires small, incremental steps. Youth need to understand that taking small steps can be an effective way to begin.

By drawing examples out of their own lives from home and from school, the youth are learning about discipleship. More important, the youth are incorporating discipleship into their lives.

### Modeling and Encouraging Good Discipleship

Jesus taught discipleship through his actions and through the use of parables. In the previous section, we saw how experiences can be used to teach discipleship, just as Jesus used parables. Actions are equally important, and the actions of the adult leaders will be on display during Covenant Discipleship Group meetings through participation in the covenant.

The greatest opportunities for modeling discipleship are found in the clauses in which both leaders and youth have difficulties. Consider the clause about reading the Bible. If the youth cannot locate their Bibles, then it does little good for the leader to tell them that he or she reads several chapters each day. In such a case, the gap is so wide between the youth and the leader that the goal as exemplified by the leader seems unattainable.

On the other hand, suppose a clause in the covenant is about praying before each meal. It is probably true that the adult is about as enthusiastic about praying before lunch at work as the youth are about praying in the school cafeteria. This is a clause where the attempts of the leader can be a helpful model for the youth. Perhaps together the leaders and youth can think of suggestions about how they can accomplish this goal together. Is the first problem just thinking of praying at lunch? Is the problem that people do not want to attract attention? Must prayer at lunch be public? Both youth and leaders can get involved in answering these and related questions.

Adult leaders also should be prepared to provide resources that might help accomplish specific goals. If reading the Bible is a problem for several youth in the group, then the leader can suggest ways to use resources to make individual efforts more strongly tied to group efforts. Devotional guides for youth, such as *Devo'Zine*, which is published by The Upper Room, a part of the General Board of Discipleship of The United Methodist Church, can be provided for youth. Suggest that they read the magazine on the same schedule, and allow some discussion of the material during each meeting.

Another approach would be to suggest a common Bible reading assignment. Select one of the Gospels and have group members read a few chapters each week. Or perhaps the church pastor could be invited to explain to the group how he or she selects passages for sermons. Each week the Covenant Discipleship Group could focus on that week's Scripture reading or Lectionary passages. Midweek telephone or e-mail reminders between group members also can be helpful.

Leaders also can work with UMYF counselors and Sunday school teachers to suggest topics, visits, or service opportunities that relate to issues raised by youth in Covenant Discipleship Group meetings.

A final suggestion concerns helping group members remember their week well enough to report accurately. Many Covenant Discipleship Group members keep a discipleship journal. Making brief notes in a journal is one way to focus on daily activities during part of meditation or prayer time. Writing out prayer concerns and questions slows down the thinking process enough to provide time for thoughts to be organized and analyzed. A brief look back at the journal immediately before a Covenant Discipleship Group meeting helps members review the details of the week so that meeting time can be used more productively.

Journal writing can help us "listen" to the promptings of the Holy Spirit. One possible covenant clause concerns listening for these promptings. Taking the time to write things out gives us time to listen as well as to process and to remember.

Journals can be notebooks that are used over a long period of time, or they can be loose sheets that are used for a single week. A sample loose-sheet journal page appears on page 60. Leaders should have loose sheets for journal pages available during Covenant Discipleship Group meetings. Even if youth have journals, they often forget them. The pages also can be prepared in advance to be used as handouts reminding youth of scheduled events or particular clauses that will be the focal point of the coming week. This is another way to integrate the covenant into their lives. Remembering is part of the journey.

## Evaluating a Covenant Discipleship Group

All groups will falter at some point along the way. Recognizing and acknowledging difficulties that arise can help solve problems before they overwhelm the group. And occasionally a group just will not work. At those times it may be harmful to the youth involved to attempt to continue those groups.

## Recognizing Signals for Change

Problems to watch for include:

- attendance problems
- failure to make progress keeping the covenant
- shortened group meetings
- unhealthy group dynamics

Lagging attendance is a clear signal of problems. Determine if the attendance problem is isolated to one or two individuals. Individual problems may be best handled away from the group. Individual attendance problems could be because of transportation or scheduling issues. Some youth may not be ready for Covenant Discipleship Groups. The fact that there is a problem tells the leader that mutual accountability has not been enough to solve the problem, and it may be time to intervene privately.

An attendance problem by several group members is usually a sign of collective problems and should be discussed as part of the group sessions. The goal for the leader is to discuss the issue without making the youth feel guilty or pressured. Acknowledge the problem and see if the youth can offer solutions. Can they help one another renew their commitments, or should the group disband? The group members need to make this decision collectively. One signal that ending the group should be considered is when the group members have no enthusiasm for solving the problem.

Failure to make progress keeping the covenant is another problem. Leaders should focus on the basics and perhaps limit the group's efforts to a single part of the covenant. Leaders should be prepared to provide active suggestions to help the youth keep the covenant. Some suggestions of this type have been discussed previously, and further ideas appear on pages 56–59. The covenant rarely needs to be rewritten as long as the clauses are general enough to allow for flexibility in interpretation. Again, involve the group members. Ask them to help decide how they can help one another determine more manageable goals.

If group meetings are too brief, the leader should try to involve the group in more meaningful discussion during the reporting. The previous section includes several examples that are appropriate for solving this problem. Try to think of new variations on the clauses, variations that might generate renewed enthusiasm in participation.

Unhealthy group dynamics can limit the effectiveness of a Covenant Discipleship Group. Personality conflicts, squabbles, and domineering personalities usually can be managed by speaking privately with the individuals involved. If several Covenant Discipleship Groups are meeting at the same time, it may be appropriate to rearrange the group assignments to avoid unhealthy dynamics.

Finally, leaders should not overlook the abilities of the youth to help solve group problems. As mentioned earlier in Part 2, today's youth often have considerable experience working in small groups. However, they may not associate those other experiences with their Covenant Discipleship Group.

Youth often compartmentalize their different group experiences and miss seeing the general ways in which those experiences agree. When group problems arise, the Covenant Discipleship Group leader can ask youth if they have had similar experiences in other kinds of groups. Through the discussion youth may be able to contribute potential solutions based on those other experiences.

## Looking to the Future

Even if the Covenant Discipleship Groups appear to be functioning well, evaluation is important. It may be beneficial to reorganize the Covenant Discipleship Groups on a regular basis. The lives of youth are built around the annual school calendar, and that is a good calendar for Covenant Discipleship Groups. As schedules change, it may be appropriate to allow some movement from group to group. Although continuity and stability aid in the development of mutual accountability, youth are not entirely in control of their schedules; and flexibility can make the difference in whether youth remain in a Covenant Discipleship Group.

Because of family schedules, it may be appropriate for the groups to discontinue meeting during summers. Start the groups in the fall and end them in late spring, if it seems appropriate. That is a good time to gather evaluations from all participants. Sample evaluation forms appear on pages 61–63.

Although some Covenant Discipleship Groups may want to stay together for a longer period, youth benefit from exposure to different people. Youth needs may change as rapidly as their bodies and minds mature, and this may create a need to remix the groups on at least a yearly basis.

Written and oral testimonies of the youth and leaders involved in Covenant Discipleship Groups also play a positive role in the evaluation process. Writing an extended response to questions about the helpfulness of Covenant Discipleship Groups is often more beneficial to the participants than filling out an evaluation form with short answers. Writing testimonies provides an opportunity for youth to evaluate the role of Covenant Discipleship Groups in their own journey of faith.

Using youth testimonials in worship is a great way to educate the congregation about Covenant Discipleship Groups as well as to build the confidence of the youth making the presentations. Testimonials are also appropriate for church newsletters or in inviting other youth to participate in Covenant Discipleship Groups.

A college senior at Hendrix College in Conway, Arkansas, who participated in a College Covenant Discipleship Group for two years wrote the following testimonial:

> *The covenant discipleship group experience has provided me with immeasurable spiritual growth and development. It seems that so often when working alone, I am unable to make the necessary commitments to myself and to God. These commitments should be an integral part of my spiritual life but so many times I seem to neglect them.*

*As part of the covenant discipleship group, I can make those commitments more easily and with greater follow-through, knowing there are others who are holding me accountable. If human nature were to be perfect, I would not need the help of others in my personal spiritual life, but since it is not, others play a vital role in keeping me on track.*

*In addition to sharing our weekly successes and failures concerning the specific covenants we have made with one another, that time we have together offers us a time for fellowship and reflection about what has happened to us during the week. During this time we are able to share personal experiences with one another.*

*With the group I have found a support structure. I have deepened existing friendships and made new ones. As I walk across campus, I am frequently met by a smiling face from the group. Even on days when it seems nothing is going right, it is amazing what a difference a friendly face can make. For anyone seeking a stronger commitment to themselves and to Christ, I would encourage joining or starting a covenant discipleship group.*

—Brandon Briery, 1995

The following testimonial was written by a seventh grade student at First United Methodist Church, in Conway, Arkansas, where the yearlong confirmation class includes a Covenant Discipleship Group component.

*My experience with the covenant of my covenant class was really something special. It taught me and those who were part of the covenant a lot. Basically our covenant group was our seventh grade confirmation class. We would break up into small groups and go over how well we did at keeping our covenant the past week. Our covenant was special to us because it was personal. Our teachers gave us a basic covenant and we were allowed to say what we wanted to keep, what we wanted to change and what we wanted to just take out all together. We could also add things that we found important. Our covenant brought us closer together and taught us a lot about ourselves, each other, and our relationship with GOD and Christ. A covenant may be hard to keep, especially for someone as young as us, but we did our best and I think we did pretty good.*

—Kassie Wilson, 1998

# Part 4

## Additional Helps

Your hands have made and fashioned me;
give me understanding that I may
learn your commandments.
**Psalm 119:73**

# References

- *Sprouts: Nurturing Children Through Covenant Discipleship*, by Edie Genung Harris and Shirley L. Ramsey (Discipleship Resources, 1995).
- "Confirmation or Graduation? Another Approach to Confirmation," by Steven W. Manskar, *Covenant Discipleship Quarterly*, Vol. 13, No. 1 (Fall 1997).
- "Covenant Discipleship and Higher Education: Hendrix College," by David Sutherland, *Covenant Discipleship Quarterly*, Vol. 10, No. 2 (Winter 1995).
- *Class Leaders: Recovering a Tradition*, by David Lowes Watson (Discipleship Resources, 1998).
- *Covenant Discipleship: Christian Formation Through Mutual Accountability*, by David Lowes Watson (Discipleship Resources, 1995).
- *The Early Methodist Class Meeting: Its Origins and Significance*, by David Lowes Watson (Discipleship Resources, 1995).
- *Forming Christian Disciples: The Role of Covenant Discipleship and Class Leaders in the Congregation*, by David Lowes Watson (Discipleship Resources, 1995).

# Resources

- *Devo'Zine* is a bimonthly devotional magazine designed for youth and written by youth and by adults who work with youth. It can be ordered by calling 800-925-6847. Church leaders can place standing orders (ten or more copies to one address) at a discounted price.
- Chrysalis is a three-day experience for youth and college students developed by The Upper Room as a youth version of the Walk to Emmaus. For information about Chrysalis, check The Upper Room website at **http://www.upperroom.org**; write to International Chrysalis Office, P.O. Box 189, Nashville, TN 37202-0189; or call 615-340-7229.
- *Covenant Discipleship Quarterly* is a quarterly newsletter for members of Covenant Discipleship groups. You can receive a free subscription by writing to *Covenant Discipleship Quarterly*, P.O. Box 840, Nashville, TN 37202-0840; by calling 615-340-7190; by faxing 615-340-7071 (Attention: JoAnn Eslinger–*Covenant Discipleship Quarterly*); or by e-mailing jeslinger@gbod.org.
- Staff members at the General Board of Discipleship can provide information on events and other resources related to Covenant Discipleship Groups. For information, check the GBOD website at **http://www.gbod.org** or write to Director, Accountable Discipleship, P.O. Box 840, Nashville, TN 37202-0840.
- The Campus Ministry Section of the General Board of Higher Education and Ministry can provide information about Covenant Discipleship Groups on college campuses. Check the United Methodist Student Movement website at **http://www.umsm.org**; write to GBHEM Campus Ministry Section, P.O. Box 871, Nashville, TN 37202-0871; phone 615-340-7415; fax 615-340-7379; or e-mail hhartley@gbhem.org.

# CONFIRMATION CLASS COVENANT

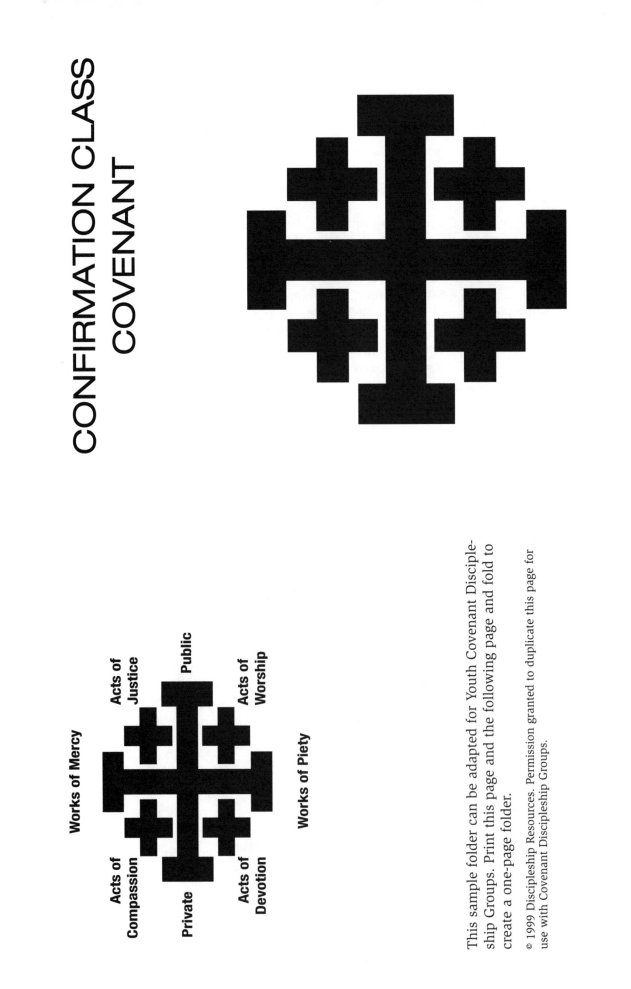

Works of Mercy

**Acts of Justice**

Public

**Acts of Worship**

**Acts of Compassion**

Private

**Acts of Devotion**

Works of Piety

This sample folder can be adapted for Youth Covenant Discipleship Groups. Print this page and the following page and fold to create a one-page folder.

# Covenant

During this time together, we are learning and growing in our faith as disciples of Jesus Christ. Under the guidance of the Holy Spirit, we pledge to follow the teachings of Jesus through the following acts of compassion, justice, worship, and devotion.

## Acts of Compassion

We will be helpful to others at home, church, and school.

We will thank someone each day.

We will participate in a service project when we can.

## Acts of Justice

We will be honest.

We will avoid sins of the tongue.

We will speak out against prejudice.

We will help recycle at home.

## Acts of Worship

We will attend worship and this group. (We will tell someone else in the group when we will be absent.)

We will attend United Methodist Youth Fellowship when possible.

We will volunteer to participate in worship.

We will take Holy Communion monthly when possible.

## Acts of Devotion

We will pray each day, including the members of this group in our prayers.

We will bless the food that we eat.

We will read our Bibles each week.

We will consider our bodies as temples of God and care for them properly.

---

## Group Covenant

We make this commitment, trusting God's grace to work in us. We know that we are children of a loving God and that if we fail, we trust God's grace to forgive us and to help us have the strength to grow in our faith.

_____

_____

_____

_____

_____

_____

_____

_____

*Signatures*

_____

*Date*

# Covenant Discipleship

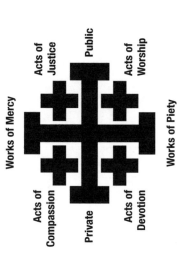

Works of Mercy

Acts of Justice

Public

Acts of Worship

Acts of Compassion

Private

Acts of Devotion

Works of Piety

This sample informational brochure can be adapted for use with College Covenant Discipleship Groups. A college logo can be added above the "Covenant Discipleship" heading. Print this page and the following page back to back to create a one-page brochure. Fold the brochure in thirds. This blank panel can be used as an address panel for mailing.

# RULE OF DISCIPLESHIP

To witness to Jesus Christ in the world and to follow his teachings through acts of compassion, justice, worship, and devotion under the guidance of the Holy Spirit.

SCHEDULE: _____

LOCATION: _____

TIME: _____

LED BY: _____

BEGINNING DATE: _____

FOR MORE INFORMATION CONTACT:

## Acts of Justice

- I will be honest and fair.
- I will not gossip.
- I will speak out against prejudice.
- I will practice good stewardship of the earth's resources.

---

I make this commitment, trusting God's grace to work in me. If I fail, I trust in God's grace to forgive me and to help me have the strength to grow in my faith.

---

## Sample Covenant

Knowing that Jesus Christ died for me and that God calls me to be a disciple of Jesus Christ, I desire to practice the following disciplines so that I might know God's love, forgiveness, guidance, and strength. I desire to grow in discipleship so that I might bear fruit for the kingdom of God.

## Acts of Devotion

- I will pray each day, including group members in my prayers.
- I will bless the food that I eat.
- I will read a chapter of the Bible each day.
- I will consider my body the temple of God and treat it as such.

## Acts of Worship

- I will worship each Sunday.
- I will take Holy Communion monthly.

## Acts of Compassion

- I will be helpful to others.
- I will prayerfully plan my day, finding a balance between work and leisure.
- I will participate in a volunteer or service project each term.

---

## What is Covenant Discipleship?

Covenant Discipleship is a way to live a life of faithful discipleship in an environment of mutual accountability and support. The Jerusalem cross shown on the cover of this brochure reminds us of the disciplines we follow as we seek to become better disciples.

## What is a Covenant Discipleship Group?

Patterned after John Wesley's early Methodist class meetings, a Covenant Discipleship Group is a group of six to eight Christians who meet briefly each week to watch over one another in love through a covenant they make with one another.

## What happens at a Covenant Discipleship Group meeting?

Group meetings open and close with prayer. The members go through the covenant together, discussing how well they followed the covenant during the past week and what their discipleship goals are for the coming week. The purpose is simply to help support and be accountable to one another.

# The General Rule of Discipleship

To witness to Jesus Christ in the world and to follow his teachings through acts of compassion, justice, worship, and devotion under the guidance of the Holy Spirit.

**Works of Mercy**

**Acts of Compassion**

**Acts of Justice**

**Private**

**Public**

**Acts of Devotion**

**Acts of Worship**

**Works of Piety**

# Commitment Form for Parents

I (We), _____, parent(s) or guardian(s) of

_____, desire to help my (our) child(ren) grow in

Christian discipleship. We pledge to walk with our child(ren) along the faith journey that

continues with the commitment to a Covenant Discipleship Group. We pledge to arrange

family priorities to help our child(ren) honor the commitment the Covenant Discipleship

Group members have made with one another. We pledge to pray for our child(ren) and

model discipleship for our child(ren) as Christ modeled discipleship for us all.


_____

Date

# Orientation Session for Parents and Youth

## Preparation
- Mail to parents and youth an information packet containing a letter of invitation giving the date and location of the orientation session, and a "Commitment Form for Parents" (page 45).
- Make announcements at UMYF meetings and other youth events.
- Display copies of "The General Rule of Discipleship" (page 44) and the sample "Youth Covenant" (page 54) on the wall of the room in which the orientation is to be held. You may want to enlarge these for easier reading.
- Mount a copy or an enlarged copy of "Youth Covenant" (page 54) on a piece of posterboard. Allow space for the youth to sign and date the poster.
- Use masking tape on the floor to represent the outline of a river that runs through the room. The outline should be about three feet wide and should run the length of the room. The "river" should not be in a straight line but should meander.
- Set up chairs (avoid placing chairs on or inside the river outline). Set up tables. Place on one the nametags and felt-tip markers, on another the refreshments, and on another the mounted copy of "Youth Covenant" and felt-tip markers.
- Decide which leaders will lead which parts of the orientation.

## Supplies
- Letters of invitation
- Copies of "Commitment Form for Parents" (page 45) to mail
- Copies or enlarged copies of "The General Rule of Discipleship" (page 44) and "Youth Covenant" (page 54) for wall display
- Copy or enlarged copy of "Youth Covenant" (page 54) to be mounted
- Copies of "Get-Acquainted Game" (page 49), one per person
- Envelopes, list of potential participants and their addresses, postage
- Posterboard
- Glue
- Masking tape
- Chairs
- Tables
- Nametags
- Felt-tip markers
- Refreshments (Refreshments need not be elaborate. Cookies, coffee, and punch are adequate.)
- Pencils
- Hymnals or other songbooks (If you have access to music on overhead transparencies, you may want to use them instead of books. You also may want to recruit someone to play the piano or guitar.)
- Blindfold

- Copies of "Commitment Form for Parents" (page 45), enough to give parents in meeting
- Small laminated copies of "Youth Covenant" (page 54) with a magnet attached to the back, enough to give youth in meeting

### Gather *(about 20 minutes)*

As parents and youth arrive, direct them to the nametags and refreshments. Give each person a copy of "Get-Acquainted Game" (page 49) and ask him or her to follow the directions printed on the page.

When everyone has arrived, ask the participants to find their seats. Welcome the youth and parents. Invite the group to join in singing several songs from a hymnal or Christian songbook. If you are using a hymnal, select contemporary hymns that are relatively easy to sing. Some possibilities from *The United Methodist Hymnal* include "El Shaddai" (123), "Thy Word Is a Lamp" (601), "I'm Goin'a Sing When the Spirit Says Sing" (333), "Lord, You Have Come to the Lakeshore" (344), and "Send Me, Lord" (497).

Offer a prayer giving thanks for those who have come and asking God's guidance in the journey that is beginning.

### Introduce the Concept of Covenant *(about 5 minutes)*

Make a short presentation on God's covenant. Review the information in Part 2 of this book to help you prepare. Use the examples of Noah, Abraham, and Moses to help the group understand the concept of God's covenant with humans. Talk about the covenant God made with these biblical people. Also talk about the willingness of these biblical people to trust God when God's requests may have sounded odd or extreme. God's requests usually involved a faith journey. Remind the group that they too are on a journey of faith.

### Play the Journey Game *(about 15 minutes)*

Ask for a volunteer who is willing to be blindfolded. Blindfold the volunteer and send him or her to one end of the river; the blindfolded youth is the traveler floating down the river in a small boat or canoe.

Ask for another volunteer to be a guide. Place the guide at the other end of the river. The goal is for the guide to verbally lead the traveler along the river to the other end. Remind group members that no journey is ever as easy as it first sounds.

Use other volunteers (youth and parents) to create distractions and obstacles. Two volunteers may join hands to create a bridge under which the traveler will pass. Another volunteer may squat to make a boulder in the river. Someone else may lie down and become a log in the river. Several others may be stationed along the banks to yell out distractions as the traveler passes by.

Then set the action in motion by having the guide yell out directions as the traveler attempts to "float" down the river while avoiding all the obstacles and distractions.

At the conclusion, ask the traveler to report how he or she felt during the trip. Then ask the guide to report his or her experience.

### Talk About Covenant Discipleship *(about 5 minutes)*

Explain briefly how Christian journeys are just as full of distractions as in the game that was just played. Just as the traveler experienced unexpected obstacles in the game, we also experience unexpected obstacles as we attempt to be faithful disciples of Jesus Christ. We need the support of others who are also on the journey to help us avoid the distractions of the "river." Covenant Discipleship Groups are a way of helping youth maintain their focus on following Jesus.

Use the information and examples in Part 2 of this book to help the youth understand the concept of mutual accountability as it relates to Covenant Discipleship.

### Introduce and Sign the Covenant *(about 15 minutes)*

Briefly describe the "Youth Covenant." Use the information in Part 3 to explain what occurs during a Youth Covenant Discipleship Group meeting. Answer questions that the youth or parents may have. Remind the parents that they are also making a commitment. Hand out copies of the "Commitment Form for Parents" and ask them to sign it.

Ask the youth to make the commitment to join a Covenant Discipleship Group by coming to the front of the room and signing the large copy of the covenant. Remind them that uncertainty is OK, and relate their uncertainty to the biblical characters talked about earlier.

Provide small laminated copies of the covenant with a magnet on the back for the participants to place on their refrigerator doors or to tie on school backpacks. The large copy can then be used as part of a display poster in the room where the Covenant Discipleship Groups will meet.

### Close

Invite everyone to join in singing a closing song such as "Sanctuary" (found in many Christian songbooks) or "Send Me, Lord" (*The United Methodist Hymnal,* 497).

# Get-Acquainted Game

Find someone to sign each of the blanks below. No person may sign your sheet more than two times.

Find someone who

1. Can name the first four books of the New Testament. _____

2. Can tell you what the word *covenant* means. _____

3. Got eight hours of sleep last night. _____

4. Has helped lead a worship service. _____

5. Has read from the Bible in the last week. _____

6. Has helped someone else this week. _____

7. Hasn't eaten any junk food today. _____

8. Has thanked God for something today. _____

9. Has invited someone else to Sunday school or another church activity. _____

10. Has participated in a service project in the last month. _____

11. Usually recycles cans or newspapers. _____

12. Isn't sure what Covenant Discipleship Groups are. _____

13. Can tell you the name of a contemporary Christian music group. _____

14. Exercises at least twice a week. _____

15. Has heard some gossip in the last week. _____

# Orientation Session for College Students

## Preparation

- Invite students involved in previous years to serve as student group leaders. Ask them to select tentative meeting times for groups. Ask them to help host the orientation session and to help make announcements and distribute brochures.
- Create a brochure for Covenant Discipleship Group ministry. Include tentative meeting times and list student leadership. (See sample brochure on pages 42–43.)
- Schedule an orientation session at a convenient time for the students. In some situations, immediately after a chapel service is a good time.
- Post copies of the brochure around campus. Update web pages.
- Make announcements at religious life events, activity fairs, and chapel services. Collect the names and addresses of students interested in more information.
- Mail copies of the brochure to the collected names.
- Arrange for the chaplain or campus minister to participate in the orientation session.
- Post enlargements of "The General Rule of Discipleship" (page 44) and the sample "College Covenant" (page 55) in the room where the orientation session is scheduled. Post separate sign-up sheets for each group, indicating the group leader and tentative meeting time.
- Set out chairs. Set up one table with nametags and felt-tip markers and one table with refreshments.

## Supplies

- Supplies to create a brochure; copies of the brochure
- Computer with Internet access
- Names and addresses of potential participants
- Envelopes, postage
- Enlarged copies of "The General Rule of Discipleship" (page 44) and "College Covenant" (page 55)
- Sign-up sheets
- Felt-tip markers
- Chairs
- Bible
- Nametags
- Refreshments

# Orientation Session Outline

**Gather** *(about 10 minutes)*

Ask the student group leaders to be present to welcome the students as they arrive and to direct them to the nametags. When everyone has arrived, ask the students to find a seat. Have one of the student group leaders offer an opening prayer.

**Scripture Reading** *(about 5 minutes)*

Ask another student group leader to read an Old Testament passage that relates to covenants. Possibilities include Genesis 9:1-17, Genesis 17:1-14, and Exodus 6:1-8. Conclude with one of the Gospel accounts of the Last Supper (Matthew 26:17-30; Mark 14:12-25; Luke 22:14-23).

**Describe the Concept of Accountable Discipleship**
*(about 10 minutes)*

Briefly introduce the concepts of discipleship, commitment, mutual accountability, and covenant relationships. Then explain Covenant Discipleship and how it relates to our Wesleyan tradition. Use the information in Parts 1 and 2 of this book to help you prepare.

**Explain Covenant Discipleship Groups** *(about 5 minutes)*

Ask student leaders to describe a Covenant Discipleship Group meeting.

**Invite Students to Join a Covenant Discipleship Group**
*(about 10 minutes)*

Introduce the student leaders and match them to their tentative Covenant Discipleship Group meeting times. Explain to the students that shortly they will have an opportunity to sign up to be in a specific group.

Close with a reminder of the role of grace in our lives of discipleship and how commitment to Christian discipleship is a response to the gift of grace.

**Organize Into Groups** *(about 15 minutes)*

Invite the students to have refreshments as they regroup themselves into Covenant Discipleship Groups with the student leaders. Ask the students to sign up for one of the groups before they leave.

# Covenant Discipleship Group Dedication Service

**Pastor:** These youth have decided that their Christian discipleship should be a focus in their lives. They stand before you today to express their desire to covenant together in a Covenant Discipleship Group. Through their covenant, which serves as a response to the call of Jesus Christ, they have agreed to meet weekly to encourage each other and to be accountable to each other as they explore the place in their lives for acts of compassion, justice, devotion, and worship.

**Youth:** Knowing that Jesus Christ died for us and that God calls us to be disciples of Jesus Christ, we desire to practice disciplines of compassion, justice, worship, and devotion so that we might know God's love, forgiveness, guidance, and strength. We desire to remain as one with Christ with the help of this covenant so that we might bear fruit for the kingdom of God.

**Parents:** We desire to help our children grow in Christian discipleship. We pledge to walk with our children along the faith journey that continues with the commitment to a Covenant Discipleship Group. We pledge to arrange family priorities to help our children honor the commitment the Covenant Discipleship Group members have made with one another. We pledge to pray for our children and to model discipleship for our children as Christ modeled discipleship for us all.

**Leaders:** We desire to model Christian discipleship with and for these youth. We pledge to lead and to support these youth as they covenant together to follow the teachings of Jesus.

**Congregation:** As members of this community of faith who covenant with one another to follow the teachings of Jesus, we honor and support these youth as they covenant together to learn and to explore the disciplines of a rich and full Christian life. We will pray for them that they might feel the love and support of this community of faith.

**Pastor:** Gracious and eternal God, we ask your blessing upon those gathered here, that they might grow in their knowledge and love for you. We know that your covenant with us never fails. Help us to be faithful to our covenant with you and with one another. Amen.

**Hymn:** "A Charge to Keep I Have" (*The United Methodist Hymnal*, 413) or "Jesu, Jesu" (*The United Methodist Hymnal*, 432)

# Confirmation Class Covenant

During confirmation we are learning and growing in our faith as disciples of Jesus Christ. Under the guidance of the Holy Spirit, we pledge to follow the teachings of Jesus through the following acts of compassion, justice, worship, and devotion.

## Acts of Compassion
We will be helpful to others at home, church, and school.
We will thank someone each day.
We will participate in a service project when we can.

## Acts of Justice
We will be honest.
We will avoid sins of the tongue.
We will speak out against prejudice when appropriate.
We will help recycle at home.

## Acts of Worship
We will attend worship and confirmation class, and we will tell someone else in the class when we will be absent.
We will attend UMYF when possible.
We will volunteer to participate in worship.
We will take Communion monthly when possible.

## Acts of Devotion
We will pray each day, including members of the confirmation class in our prayers.
We will bless the food that we eat.
We will read our Bibles each week.
We will consider our bodies as temples of God and will care for them properly.

We make this commitment, trusting God's grace to work in us. We know that we are children of a loving God and that if we fail, we trust God's grace to forgive us and to help us have the strength to grow in our faith.

# Youth Covenant

Knowing that Jesus Christ died for us and that God calls us to be disciples of Jesus Christ, we desire to practice the following disciplines together so that we might know God's love, forgiveness, guidance, and strength. Under the guidance of the Holy Spirit, we pledge to follow the teachings of Jesus through the following acts of compassion, justice, worship, and devotion.

## Acts of Compassion

We will be helpful to others at home, church, and school.
We will thank someone each day.
We will participate in a service project when we can.

## Acts of Justice

We will be honest.
We will avoid sins of the tongue.
We will speak out against prejudice when appropriate.
We will act responsibly in our relationship with friends.
We will help recycle at home.

## Acts of Worship

We will attend worship regularly and volunteer to participate in the service regularly.
We will attend Sunday school and UMYF when possible.
We will take Communion monthly when possible.

## Acts of Devotion

We will attend our Covenant Discipleship Group meetings.
We will pray each day, including Covenant Discipleship Group members in our prayers.
We will bless the food that we eat, including praying before meals.
We will read a chapter of the Bible each day.
We will consider our bodies as temples of God and will care for them properly.

We make this commitment, trusting God's grace to work in us. We know that we are children of a loving God and that if we fail, we trust God's grace to forgive us and to help us have the strength to grow in our faith.

# College Covenant

Knowing that Jesus Christ died for me and that God calls me to be a disciple of Jesus Christ, I desire to practice the following disciplines so that I might know God's love, forgiveness, guidance, and strength. I desire to make God's will my own and to be obedient to it. I desire to remain in Christ with the help of this covenant so that I might bear fruit for the kingdom of God.

## Acts of Devotion

I will pray each day, including the covenant group members in my prayers and blessing the food that I eat.

I will read at least one chapter of the Bible each day.

I will consider my body the temple of God and treat it as such.

## Acts of Worship

I will worship each Sunday and take Communion at least once a month, unless I am prevented.

I will listen to and respond to God's promptings.

## Acts of Compassion

I will be conscious of other people's needs.

I will try not to say things that will hurt other people.

I will participate in a volunteer or service project each term.

## Acts of Justice

I will be honest and fair.

I will not gossip.

I will speak out against prejudice when I see or hear it.

I will practice good stewardship of the earth's resources.

I make this commitment, trusting God's grace to work in me. If I fail, I trust God's grace to forgive me and to help me have the strength to grow in my faith.

# Acts of Compassion

Following are some concrete suggestions for how Acts of Compassion can be lived out. Use these as a springboard for discussion to help youth envision additional ways that they can live out this clause in their covenant.

## We will be helpful to others at home, church, and school.
- Do chores at home without complaining.
- Stay after a meeting at church to straighten the room.
- Help another student with homework.
- Help your siblings with one of their chores.
- Pick up trash along your street.
- Open a door for someone else whenever you can.
- Pick a day when group members can be available before a church function to greet people in the parking lot and to offer to open doors and carry packages.

## We will thank someone each day.
Goals that group members can try for a week at a time:
- Thank a family member each day.
- Thank a friend each day.
- Thank a teacher each day.
- Thank a staff member at school each day (janitors, bus drivers, and secretaries).
- Thank, or compliment, someone you do not know each day.
- Thank, or compliment, a young child each day.

## We will participate in a service project when we can.
- Pick fresh fruit at a local orchard and take the fruit to a nursing home or homeless shelter.
- Ask your pastor for the names of older people in your congregation who are limited in their ability to leave their homes. Arrange a time to visit or to send cards.
- Volunteer to help with an after-school tutoring program.
- Volunteer with an adult literacy program.
- Organize a prayer chain in your congregation that people can contact when they have prayer concerns.
- Collect personal hygiene items for a homeless shelter.
- Help with a building ministry such as Habitat for Humanity.
- Look for ways to include service projects in groups you already belong to but which do not usually get involved in service projects. Examples include your school clubs, music organizations such as choir or band, and family reunions.
- Ask your pastors or church leaders to include youth options in adult service opportunities planned by your local church.

# Acts of Justice

Following are some concrete suggestions for how Acts of Justice can be lived out. Use these as a springboard for discussion to help youth envision additional ways they can live out this clause in their covenant.

## We will be honest.

Have discussions in your Covenant Discipleship Group about the following questions:
- What are some situations when you are most likely to avoid being truthful?
- Do you ever find yourself avoiding certain issues because you are afraid of the consequences of being truthful?
- Have you ever been in a situation where honesty was used as a weapon?

Invite members of particular professions to talk with the group about honesty in their professions. Examples include lawyers, ministers, physicians, or business owners.

## We will avoid sins of the tongue.

Have discussions in your Covenant Discipleship Group about the following questions:
- Do you use language differently depending on who is around you?
- Is it OK to swear in private but not in public?
- Can gossip be a "sin of the tongue"?
- Is gossip ever good?
- Can sarcasm be a "sin of the tongue"?

## We will speak out against prejudice when appropriate.
- Avoid laughing when others tell jokes that involve prejudice.
- Don't listen to music that puts others down.
- Pledge to be friendly toward someone who is outside your circle of friends.
- Visit a worship service that is different from the ones with which you are familiar.

## We will act responsibly in our relationships with friends.
- Pledge to remind each other (later and privately) when you see each other not acting responsibly. Acting responsibly can include your actions concerning smoking, using alcohol, swearing, lying, trashing someone else verbally, and driving safely.

## We will help recycle at home.
- Call a recycling center and learn what can be recycled in your community.
- Help educate family members about what can be recycled.
- Volunteer to sort family recyclables.
- Sew cloth napkins for family meals.
- Think of ways to reduce trash from sack lunches.

# Acts of Worship

Following are some concrete suggestions for how Acts of Worship can be lived out. Use these as a springboard for discussion to help youth envision additional ways they can live out this clause in their covenant.

## We will attend worship regularly and volunteer to participate in the service regularly.
- Volunteer to help at a Communion service.
- Volunteer to serve as ushers.
- Volunteer to fold bulletins.
- Volunteer to straighten the sanctuary after worship.
- Commit to paying better attention in worship.
- Commit to singing the hymns and reading the Scripture passages used in worship.
- Ask your adult leaders or worship committee to provide music, drama, or dance opportunities for worship services.

## We will attend Sunday school and UMYF when possible.
- Form an e-mail group to remind one another of UMYF events.
- Volunteer to help plan a Sunday school session or UMYF activity.
- Volunteer to help lead your Covenant Discipleship Group.
- Pledge with a friend to help encourage each other's attendance.
- Help arrange rides to and from church activities for friends without transportation.

## We will take Communion monthly when possible.
- Learn about the opportunities that are available to you and your group for participating in Communion services.
- Ask your group leader or pastor to help provide alternative Communion opportunities on occasion.
- Visit other worship services or invite speakers to help you explore the many different ways Christians organize Communion services.

# Acts of Devotion

**We will attend our Covenant Discipleship Group meetings.**
- Arrange to share rides to group meetings.
- Call friends who miss group meetings to say hello and that you missed them.
- If you know you will miss a group meeting, call another group member and explain that you will be absent.

**We will pray each day, including group members in our prayers.**
- When you are stopped at a traffic light, say a brief prayer for occupants of other cars.
- When you are in a line, pray for others in line or pray for the employee dealing with the line (cashier, ticket taker, and so forth).
- When you see friends, thank God for their friendship.
- Keep a prayer journal for listing prayer requests.
- Read a devotional from a resource like *Devo'Zine* or The Upper Room each day.
- Sign up for an online or e-mail devotional list.

**We will bless the food that we eat, including praying before meals.**
- Volunteer to help your family learn new prayers to say or sing at meals.
- Develop a family grace that can be said together before family meals.
- Remember that quick silent prayers count! You do not have to call attention to yourself.
- Use your Covenant Discipleship Group friends as visual reminders to pray at meals.
- Remember that blessing your meal does not have to occur before you begin eating. It is more important at first just to remember to pray.
- Think about your prayer as a conversation with God. Use your prayer time as an alternative to watching television or listening to music while you eat.

**We will read a chapter of the Bible each day.**
- Learn about the Lectionary and use the suggested passages as a guide for reading.
- Use a devotional guide such as *Devo'Zine* to help you decide what Scripture to read.
- Explore different ways to read your Bible:
    Try reading a particular book one chapter at a time.
    Try opening your Bible and reading a randomly chosen chapter or psalm.
    Try using a word search device on your computer to select interesting passages.
    Try using a devotional guide, a directed reading guide, or a study Bible.
    Try selecting common passages for the group members to read at the same time.
    Try reading from different translations or versions of the Bible.
    If you read another language, try reading the Bible in that language.

**We will consider our bodies as temples and care for them properly.**
- Keep track of the food you eat for a week and compare it to nutritional guidelines.
- Find a training partner (perhaps someone in the Covenant Discipleship Group) who will exercise with you on a regular basis.
- Consider the effects of smoking and alcohol usage on your body.
- Look for ways to find a balance between work and play.

# My Covenant Journal

Use these journal pages to help you record and monitor how you are keeping your covenant. Use the back of the page to write or draw your reflections about your discipleship for the week.

| | Acts of Compassion | Acts of Justice | Acts of Worship | Acts of Devotion |
|---|---|---|---|---|
| **Sunday** | | | | |
| **Monday** | | | | |
| **Tuesday** | | | | |
| **Wednesday** | | | | |
| **Thursday** | | | | |
| **Friday** | | | | |
| **Saturday** | | | | |

# Evaluation Form
# for Covenant Discipleship
# Group Members

How has the Covenant Discipleship Group experience helped you grow in discipleship?

_____

_____

What was the best part of your Covenant Discipleship Group experience? _____

_____

How would you change the program to make Covenant Discipleship Groups better?

_____

How do you feel about the following parts of the Covenant Discipleship Group program:

Orientation Session    _____

Covenant _____

Leaders _____

Group Service Projects _____

Group Worship Time _____

*Devo'Zine* or other devotional materials _____

Journal _____

Do you want to continue being a part of a Covenant Discipleship Group? _____

Would you recommend Covenant Discipleship Groups to your friends? Why? _____

_____

# Evaluation Form for Youth Covenant Discipleship Group Leaders

How has the Covenant Discipleship Group experience helped you grow in discipleship?

_____

_____

How has the Covenant Discipleship Group experience helped youth grow in discipleship?

_____

What was the best part of your Covenant Discipleship Group experience? _____

_____

Do you believe that you were an effective leader? Explain. _____

_____

How can the following parts of the program be made more effective:

Orientation Session _____

Covenant _____

Leaders _____

Group Service Projects _____

Group Worship Time _____

*Devo'Zine* and other devotional materials _____

Journal _____

Do you want to continue leading a Youth Covenant Discipleship Group? Why? _____

_____

Would you recommend Covenant Discipleship to others? Why? _____

_____

# Evaluation Form for Parents

Did your youth enjoy being part of a Covenant Discipleship Group? Explain. _____

_____

How has the Covenant Discipleship Group experience helped your youth grow in discipleship?

_____

As a parent, what was the most effective part of the Youth Covenant Discipleship experience?

_____

How would you change the program to make Covenant Discipleship Groups better for the youth?

_____

How would you change the program to make Youth Covenant Discipleship Groups more convenient for parents? _____

_____

How do you feel about the following parts of the Youth Covenant Discipleship Group program:

Orientation Session _____

Covenant _____

Leaders _____

Scheduling _____

Do you want your youth to continue being part of a Covenant Discipleship Group? _____

Would you recommend Covenant Discipleship Groups to other parents of youth? Why?

_____

Are you interested in joining a Covenant Discipleship group? Why? _____

_____

# Accountable Discipleship Canopy

Youth and College Covenant Discipleship Groups are part of a larger ministry of accountable discipleship. The diagram below indicates a sampling of the many groups and settings that fall within the canopy of accountable discipleship. If you are interested in finding out more about any of the groups listed below, contact the Office of Accountable Discipleship, General Board of Discipleship, P.O. Box 840, Nashville, TN 37202-0840.